Coaltowns of West Virginia

A Pictorial Recollection

Coaltowns of West Virginia

A Pictorial Recollection

Fayette

Raleigh

Wyoming

Boone

Logan

Mercer

Mary Legg Stevenson

Quarrier Press

Charleston, WV 25301

Copyright 1998 by Quarrier Press

All Rights Reserved

First Edition

July 1998

Library of Congress #98-066203

ISBN# 1-891852-01-9

Design: Rita Damous Kee

Front Cover Photo: By William O. Trevey, Courtesy Fred Frisk

Color Tinting: Pat Dodd, Photographic Production Services

Printed in USA

TABLE OF CONTENTS

PAGE

ACKNOWLEDGEMENTS VII
INTRODUCTION VIII
ALLOY 1
AMIGO 2
BEARDS FORK 3
BESOCO 7
BEURY 8
BRAEHOLM (FANCO) 11
BUD 12
CALORIC 14
CAPERTON 19
DRY CREEK 20
EAST GULF 21
FAITH 27
FAYETTE 29
FIRECO 32
GLEN FERRIS 33
GLEN ROGERS 34
GLEN WHITE 42
HELEN 44
ITMANN 54
JONBEN 55
LILLYBROOK 57
LOOKOUT 59
MABEN 63
McALPIN 64
MEAD POCA 71
MONTECARLO 77
MORDUE 80
MORRISON (GLEN MORRISON) 86
NALLEN 87
PAGE 90
PEMBERTON 91
PHILLIPS 92
PICKSHIN 94
QUINNIMONT 102
RALCO 104
RALEIGH 111
RHODELL 116
SLAB FORK 127
STOTESBURY 131
SYLVESTER 133

TABLE OF CONTENTS (cont.)

PAGE

TOMMY CREEK 135
TRALEE 137
VANWOOD 148
WHIPPLE 154
WINDING GULF 155
WINONA 157
PAWAMA 162
TODAY IN THE COAL FIELDS 164
BIBLIOGRAPHY 167
ABOUT THE AUTHOR 168
INDEX 169

ACKNOWLEDGEMENTS

I consider it very fortunate that long ago an engineer from Merrill Engineering Company, in Beckley, West Virginia, took pictures at various coal mining operations, carefully labeling and saving the negatives. Now some eighty odd years later, we can see what life and work was like in some of the old coal towns; towns that are not even on the maps now.

Ernest M. Merrill founded Merrill Engineering in 1906. He was joined by J. M. Ferguson, who invited Lauren A. Gates to become associated with them in 1920. In 1928 Merrill sold his interest, and the firm became the partnership Ferguson-Gates. It operated under this name until the death of Ferguson in 1943, when L. A. Gates became the sole owner. Later Leslie C. Gates joined his father in the firm. Upon the death of the elder Gates, Leslie became head of the firm. The firm was sold to EBASCO of New York, and in the change of hands, EBASCO sold the mining department to Thomas Gales, which became Gales Engineering Company.

The pictures in this publication came down through the years to Thomas Gales, who in turn gave them to the author. History was recorded, saved and passed to us today in the form of these pictures.

My deepest thanks and appreciation to Thomas Gales, P.E., for the gift of about one hundred and fifty negatives, which were used to make the photographs in this book. Thanks to Fred Frisk of Mount Hope for developing the photos for me. I am also indebted to Mr. Gales for the pictures in my first book *From Affinity to Winding Gulf* (1989), and many of the photos in *From Ameagle to Wingrove* (1990), my second book. Through his gift he has allowed me to share these pictures with thousands of readers.

Many of the photographs in this book were loaned by various persons, and credit is given with each photo. I appreciate the use of the photos, and for the stories everyone shared with me. Thanks to Mr. Gene Hooker, who helped me identify the McAlpin pictures, and to John (Jack) Feller, who helped me with the Mullens area pictures.

Many thanks to Emily Hudnall of Kingsport, Tennessee, for the pencil drawing on the title page.

I am grateful to my husband, Dan, for his support, encouragement, and for the many miles he has driven me to gather information for this book.

Somewhere in Southern West Virginia

Introduction

In the late 19th century, the advent of coal mining on a large scale changed the face of the West Virginia mountains forever. It is doubtful that the coal industry would have become as profitable as it did, as quickly, without the growing emergence of the railroad in less settled parts of the state. Because of the growing coal industry, more people moved into the state, new towns sprang up, and fortunes were earned almost overnight. At the same time, people perished in dark mines, sometimes earning slave wages, and were forced to shop in company stores. In addition to irrevocable changes made to the state's economy, the coal industry made drastic alterations to the landscape. As we approach the twenty-first century, coal mining is still West Virginia's largest industry. Interestingly enough, it is largely because of the pristine and mountainous parts of our state that tourism ranks second, only to coal. It is a matter of opinion whether, overall, the effect of coal mining on the state has been good or bad.

Because of increased technology and federal regulations, the physical act of coal mining is safer than ever before. In the past, forests were cut and left to grow back on their own; now young trees are planted to replace the old. At one time lands were mined and the debris was left for Mother Nature. Now state and federal regulations govern altering the topographical face of our state.

Because I am a native of the West Virginia coalfields, I have had an ongoing fascination with the coal industry and the changes it has wrought on our state. In addition to this book, I have published two others that are pictorial collections of early coal mining in West Virginia: *From Affinity to Winding Gulf* (1989) and *From Ameagle to Wingrove* (1990).

It has been my good fortune that I came into the possession of hundreds of photographs depicting West Virginia during the coal boom. Many of the photographs in this book date from the late teens and early twenties of this century. Others date from as late as the 1960's. My main goal in writing these three books is to preserve history, and demonstrate a way of mining coal that is almost forgotten. I believe that passing stories down in both oral and written form is a critical way to preserve and understand our heritage. As I grow older, my heritage and memories become more and more meaningful. I think this is true for many West Virginians. This book is a pictorial history of a way of life that no longer exists.

In Raleigh County, the first lumber company arrived, soon to be followed by the trains and coal companies. Towns appeared out of nowhere, and became ghost towns a few short decades later. In Fayette County, the C & O main line became accessible in 1872; and the mining of bituminous coal in the county took off. By 1888, Fayette County mines were the largest coal producers in West Virginia. In Wyoming County, H. H. Rogers' Virginian railway arrived in 1909, and Wyoming County mines began shipping coal in earnest. But when the use of the land's vast resources waned, sales decreased, or workers demanded increased benefits, the coal companies pulled out. The towns grew obsolete, and the communities soon died. This is what happened to most of the communities covered in this book. What was once a vibrant, thriving community is now not even a name on a map.

We could drive to what was once the town of McAlpin, and not be able to see even the remains of what at one time was a booming coal town. Seventy years ago, Stotesbury and Slab Fork were towns of several hundred families, with churches, community centers, and doctors. Now only a few residential houses remain. To many West Virginians, this is where the desire to preserve our history begins. Historical photographs let people re-live their own and their parents' childhoods, show their children where Grandpa worked, and re-member the hometown ball games and silent movie shows.

The coal companies are difficult to trace, because they changed owners so many times, and the records are sketchy. It has been said that the companies changed hands so often that no one but the owners themselves knew the owner. The best source I found, which reported on the activity of all mines in the state, was the West Virginia Annual Report of the Department of Mines.

The demand for coal during World Wars I and II brought growth and prosperity to the state. But as the demand declined after the wars, many owners closed their mines and returned to their home states of Pennsylvania, New York, or Ohio. A small portion of the big coal barons were local men. The Caperton brothers, of Slab Fork, spent their lives in West Virginia. Mr. E. C. Minter came to Raleigh County as a young man, and spent his life here, active in mining as well as church and civic affairs. Major W. P. Tams came to West Virginia as a young man from Virginia, and lived here his entire life. I feel the greatest kinship to those men who came to West Virginia, worked the mines, loved our people, and stayed to enjoy the spectacular beauty of southern West Virginia.

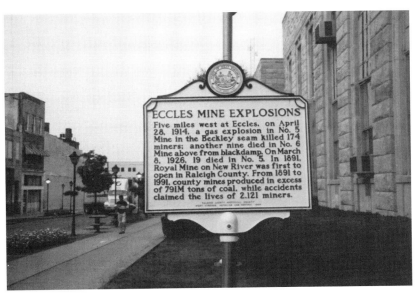

Historical Marker erected on Raleigh County Courthouse Square. The marker was erected to commemorate the Eccles Mine explosions and all the miners who lost their lives in mine accidents from 1891-1991. Erected by the Raleigh County Historical Society.

ALLOY - Fayette County: Located on the Kanawha River in the Falls district. First named "Carbon," it was changed to "Boncar" (Carbon rearranged) in 1920, to avoid confusion with Mt. Carbon, which is nearby. The name Alloy was chosen by the Electro Metallurgical Company, which owned the village and plant.

The Willson Aluminum Company started at Kanawha Falls, also known as Glen Ferris, in 1898. The company was sold to the Electro Metallurgical Company in 1907. Company officials had the plant's name changed to Union Carbide Metals Company in 1959.

Business increased in the early 1920's and in 1926, Union Carbide purchased the land they needed to build a new plant facility at Boncar. In 1929 the mines, owned by the West Virginia Eagle Coal Company, were bought by EMCO. This mine furnished coal for the Union Carbide plant until it was completely worked out.

COURTESY JAMES W. YOUELL

Tipple, Amigo
Coal Company.

AMIGO - Raleigh County: Named for Amigo Smokeless Coal Company which was established in 1914 by Dr. Joseph A. Wood. Amigo coal was low-volatile coal that produced a very low ash content and was in great demand. At one time the company operated three mines. The mines operated under Dr. Wood, and later by his sons, until February 1945 when they were sold to E. C. Minter Coal Company. The name changed in July of the same year. In March of 1948, the company was again sold, this time to the Lillybrook Coal Company, and the name was changed to Amigo Smokeless Coal.

By 1950 Amigo Smokeless was mining about 1,300 tons per day. In 1949 they reached production of 177,000 tons in 159 working days. Before mining came to the area, the lands forming Amigo were home to an active logging business.

Miners' homes, Amigo.

View of Beards Fork.
PHOTOGRAPHS OF BEARDS FORK COURTESY OF FLORENCE PAINTER

BEARDS FORK - Fayette County: Located on Loup Creek seven and a half miles from Deepwater on a branch line of the Virginian railroad. The name was derived from an old prospector and ginseng hunter, Mr. Beard, who made his way up this valley through the dense forest, camped under a cliff, hunted wild animals, and dug ginseng.

Elkhorn Piney Coal Company, Loup Creek Colliery, Koppers Coal Company, and Eastern Gas & Fuel all had active mines up and down the rugged mountains that formed Beards Fork.

Scrip office with the "Grill" in background.

BEARDS FORK

Beards Fork grade school.

Boys enjoying the summer in front of the "Grill."

BEARDS FORK

The scrip office and bridge path to the company store.

The doctor's office and the Princess Theater.

Bob Thompson and Stark Amick on a mine motor near the mine entrance.

BEARDS FORK

Koppers General Store.

The remains of the company store - 1997.

The company store and office.

BESOCO - Raleigh County: Beckley Smokeless Coal Company was opened by E. C. Minter in 1915. The name 'Besoco' was derived from the initials of the Company. By 1917 Beckley Smokeless was operating two drift mines of the Beckley coal seam, producing 53,750 tons of coal. E. C. Minter was superintendent, and D. W. Miller was mine foreman. The coal was shipped on the Virginian Railway.

Tipple and incline, Beckley Smokeless Coal Company.

7

BEURY

BEURY - Fayette County: Lies near Fire Creek on the New River in the Sewell Mountain district, and was named for Colonel Joseph L. Beury. A pioneer coal operator, Beury came to Fayette County in 1872, and helped organize the first coal company in Fayette County, the New River Coal Company. He shipped the first coal from the New River area after completion of the C & O Railway in 1873. Beury helped organize the Fire Creek mines in 1876 and the Mill Creek Coal & Coke Company.

Colonel Beury married Julia A. Forbes in Pennsylvania, and soon after brought her to the wilds of the New River. At seventeen she left a comfortable home to follow her husband into the wilderness. They lived in a log cabin for about five years at Fire Creek, when the nearest railroad was at White Sulphur Springs. The couple next moved to Hawks Nest, where provisions were available only once a month. From Hawks Nest they moved to Caperton, and from there to Beury.

In 1881, Colonel Beury opened a mine at Echo, one mile east of Fire Creek. The name Echo was changed later to Beury. In 1885 the Colonel moved into his new home at Beury, living there until his death in 1903.

Company store at Beury - 1909.
COURTESY MRS. PAULINE STONE

Warren Lodge No. 109 was chartered in Thurmond in 1896. This building was erected in Beury in 1903.

BEURY

Small town community growth was important to the owners of most of the mines. The owners needed men to mine their coal, which entailed the necessity of providing living quarters for families. To encourage men to bring their families, the owners would build community buildings, build or support a church, provide a doctor, and help form social organizations.

Colonel Beury, a charter member of Warren Lodge No. 109, A. F. & A. M. at Thurmond, entertained a notion to build a lodge at Beury. A building committee, consisting of G. H. Caperton (later of Slab Fork), John Laing (McAlpin), and A. S. Guthrie, were named to oversee the construction of this lodge hall. It was completed in 1903 and used until destroyed in a fire in August 30, 1925. Mr. W. H. Warren was Worshipful Master, John Laing was Senior Warden, and Augustis S. Guthrie, Junior Warden. The lodge merged with Mt. Hope in 1963 to become McDonald-Warren Lodge No. 103.

The ruins of a once beautiful coal baron's mansion.
Today Beury is one of many vanished towns in the coalfields.

BRAEHOLM (FANCO) - Logan County:

In 1922 the Amherst Coal Company No. 4 operated a drift mine in the Island Creek coal bed and used the Braeholm post office. A. S. J. Hopkins was superintendent, and Thomas Quinn was the mine foreman.

These are the only photographs in this book documenting Logan County. There are few records of these rapidly disappearing, or vanished, coal towns.

Amherst Coal Company No. 4
COURTESY LOUISE MCGRAW

Row of homes in Fanco.

Our English Heritage
A great many of our early coal operators came from England, Scotland, and Wales, either directly or one generation away. In Great Britain the avoirdupois weight is 2,400 pounds and equals one long ton. In the United States a ton is 2,000 pounds, and is sometimes called a short ton.

BUD - Wyoming County: Named for Bud Adams, who had a logging camp on Barker Creek.

A view of Thermo Pocahontas Coal Company at Bud.
Women crossing the railroad tracks to get to the company store.

Miners' homes.

BUD

Tipple and incline.

By 1917 Thermo Pocahontas Coal Company was operating five mines and mined 19,908 tons; in 1918 it produced 75,110 tons. In 1924 Thermo mined 94,424 tons and employed 50 men.

One of the most important by-products of West Virginia coal has been coke, which in 1880 began to replace charcoal in the manufacture of steel. Oven gas, tar, light oil, and ammonia are other primary by-products.

Coal by-products are used in numerous items, including saccharin, perfumes, aspirin, Vaseline, vanillin (the chief fragrant ingredient in vanilla), and dyes. Researchers have discovered certain rare minerals in coal, among them germanium, a non-metal (metalloid) element used in the electronics industry. Even oil and gas can be produced synthetically from coal; although the conversion costs are high.

CALORIC - Wyoming County:

The Smith Pocahontas Coal Company, one of the J. C. Sullivan interests, opened in Caloric in 1917. This was a drift mine, and A. K. Minter was superintendent. In 1918 they mined 29,950 tons of coal. In 1919 they mined 40,800 tons, but by 1924 production had dropped to 14,535 tons.

At one time the Raleigh Fire Creek Coal Company, Raleigh Wyoming Coal Company, Mead Pocahontas Coal Company, Pickshin Coal Company, Barkers Creek Coal Company, Smith Pocahontas Coal Company, Harty Coal Company and Wood-Sullivan Coal Company, were all part of the J. C. Sullivan interests. Mr. Sullivan's office building and his residence were located in Mead Poca. Caloric and Mead Poca are now part of west Mullens.

Company store and office.

Caloric dwelling.

CALORIC

A view of Caloric with a boxcar near the company store.

Miners' homes on the hillside in Caloric.

CALORIC

Caloric homes, now a part of Mullens.

A view of Caloric.

EAST GULF

One of the larger homes, for a company official.

A nice house with stone foundation.

EAST GULF

Drift mouth with rock wall formation.

The motor and mine car repair shop.

EAST GULF

Car repair shop.

The supply house with discarded drums.

EAST GULF

Mine car of coal waiting to be dumped.

Incline from the mine above the railroad tracks.

FAITH

Faith Smokeless Coal Company tipple.

FAITH - Wyoming County: Faith Smokeless Coal Company formed in 1926 under the leadership of C. H. Mead.

Faith houses with mine cars in foreground.

FAITH

Faith Smokeless Coal Company drift mouth.

C. H. Mead drilled the first gas well in Wyoming County on Milam Fork in 1920 for the Ravencliffe Development Company. Mead was the president and general manager. Natural gas from the well was soon made available for domestic use.

FAYETTE - Fayette County: From 1908-1913 Manufacturers & Consumers Coal Company operated a mine called "Newlyn". This was a drift mine located on the main line of the C & O Railroad, four miles east of Hawks Nest and one mile west of Fayette Station. The Sewell seam had a thickness of about three feet; the roof was slate. Ventilation was produced by an eight-foot Thayer exhaust fan. In 1912 they mined 39,988 tons of coal and employed 60 miners. The superintendent was P. H. Henry; and James W. Sims was mine foreman.

Also in Fayette was the Michigan Coal Company, which operated a drift mine along the New River and on the main line of the C & O Railway, about 4 miles from Hawks Nest. The Michigan mine (prior to 1901 called the Masterson mine) operated until about 1920. The new owner was the New River Export Smokeless Coal Company.

In 1903 James Boone was superintendent of the Michigan mine, and Val Backman was mine boss. The pick miners were paid from 55 to 60 cents per ton, and those loading after the machines received 27 cents per long ton. All the coal was hauled by mules. The mine employed fifty men.

FAYETTE - Manufacturers & Consumers Coal Company. COURTESY LOUISE MCGRAW

FAYETTE - Michigan Coal Company.   COURTESY LOUISE MCGRAW

31

FIRECO - Raleigh County: Leckie Fire Creek Coal Company and Douglas Coal Company. In 1917 Leckie & Douglas employed 64 men and mined 33,513 tons of coal.

Store and office - Leckie & Douglas.

Club house - Lillybrook No. 2.

Lillybrook Coal Company, also in Fireco, employed 81 men and produced 16,513 tons of coal in 1917.

GLEN ROGERS

A view of the plant from upstream.

The plant and shops.

GLEN ROGERS

Loaded Virginian Railway coal cars with a "dinkey Engine" on a side track.

Dwellings on Main Laurel Branch.

GLEN ROGERS

View of the Negro section of town. In the second row,
notice the attached row of houses.

Another view on Main Laurel branch.

GLEN WHITE - Raleigh County:

Mr. E. E. White obtained a lease from the Beaver Coal Company, forming the E. E. White Coal Company, and opened the Glen White and Stotesbury mines in 1909 and 1910. By 1918 they were the county's largest producers with 636,583 tons.

Mr. White built quality housing for his workers and their families, along with a large company store, stone office building, churches, brick school houses, and a hall that housed a confectionary and theater. Glen White and Stotesbury were considered two of the better coal communities.

The stately mansion that Mr. White had built for his family in 1906, sat proudly on a hill overlooking his town. Listed in the National Register of Historic Places, this house was damaged by fire June 29, 1996.

In 1925 Mr. White sold the mines and retired to Pennsylvania.

Company store building - E.E. White Coal Company.

GLEN WHITE

The auditorium in the recreation hall.

Loaded mine cars.

HELEN - Raleigh County:

Located on Winding Gulf in the Slab Fork district. Helen was named after the daughter of G. W. Stevens, President of the C & O Railroad. East Gulf Coal Company, under the direction of Western Pocahontas Coal Company, had their operations at Helen. By 1921 East Gulf was running three mines of the Beckley seam and producing 501,973 tons. Mr. P. C. Thomas was superintendent, and Henry Blake was mine foreman.

East Gulf Coal Company, store and office.

Overlooking Helen. The clubhouse can be seen in center back. This picture was probably taken before 1916 as only the Virginian track is visible. Part of the incline and tipple of East Gulf Coal Company are in the background.

HELEN

Clubhouse.

Superintendent's home.

Amusement hall.

HELEN

A row of miners' homes, with the superintendent's house to the rear and company store on the right. A team of horses and wagon share the road with a car.

Clothes on the line, a convertible car, and a screened front porch on the big house. The clubhouse is in the right background.

HELEN

East Gulf Coal Company tipple.

Tipple - where the mine cars were pulled and "tipped" over to load the railroad coal cars.

HELEN

Row of miners' homes built along the railroad track with a water tank on the hill.

Multiple housing.

HELEN

Incline from the mine opening.

Preparation plant (tipple) with inclines to right and left.

HELEN

Drift mine opening.

Car and motor repair shop.

JONBEN - Raleigh County: Wilton Smokeless Coal Company. In 1921, their mine, "Bacontown" produced 44,262 tons and employed 50 men.

Home of the store manager.

Miners' homes at Jonben.

JONBEN

Old residential home on Wilton Smokeless Coal Company property.

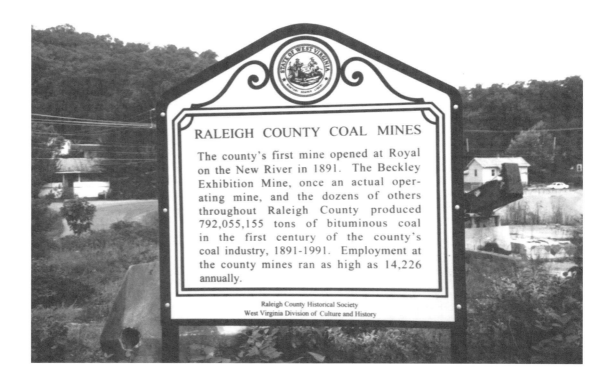

RALEIGH COUNTY COAL MINES

The county's first mine opened at Royal on the New River in 1891. The Beckley Exhibition Mine, once an actual operating mine, and the dozens of others throughout Raleigh County produced 792,055,155 tons of bituminous coal in the first century of the county's coal industry, 1891-1991. Employment at the county mines ran as high as 14,226 annually.

Raleigh County Historical Society
West Virginia Division of Culture and History

LILLYBROOK

LILLYBROOK - Raleigh County: The Lillybrook Coal Company was organized by Prince E. Lilly and his son-in-law, John B. Hornbrook. Mr. Lilly was born in Raleigh in 1861, the son of John A. Lilly. Mr. Lilly also dealt extensively in timber and real estate. In 1917, Lillybrook Coal Company No. 2 employed 76 men and mined 16,513 tons of coal.

Store and office.

Residence of the superintendent.

LILLYBROOK

Home of the general manager.

Residence of store manager.

LOOKOUT

LOOKOUT - Fayette County: Located on Keeney Creek in the Nuttall district, on the old James River and Kanawha Turnpike road. Lookout is at the crossroads going south to Nuttallburg on New River, and north to Nallen on Meadow River. Formerly named "De-Kalb", "Pleasant Hill", and "Locust Lane". The present name derives from the fact that the spot was used both by the Indians and white men as a lookout point during conflicts.

J. F. Cavendish started the town of Lookout around 1893 when he built a large store on the turnpike, opened a coal mine, and built ten or more houses for the coal miners. In 1896, David Wallace Boone and his brothers bought the Cavendish coal mine and property.

D. W. Boone was credited with being the planner, architect, and builder of the town of Lookout. The Methodist church was built in 1893, and the Baptist church in 1897. The town also had a bakery, theater, four stores, a garage, two restaurants, and a drug store. Mr. Boone built a hotel that contained 31 rooms, had electric lights, and hot and cold running water. The hotel sat on a hill looking across a small valley to Mr. Boone's home, which was a beautiful two-story house, with double porches around three sides, a stable, and a manicured lawn. The hotel burned in 1930, but the Boone home still stands and is in private hands. Its owners are working to restore the house to its original beauty.

In 1908, the WV Department of Mines listed that Lookout Coal & Coke Company had an "outside coke yard" and employed 6 people. The company also operated a Sewell seam drift mine with superintendent D. W. Boone, and mine foreman Andrew Boone. By 1909 they employed 40 pick miners, 3 mine machines for inside work and five outside workers. They worked an average of 251 days in 1909. Mr. Boone lost this company during the Depression.

D. W. Boone and his brothers operated their mines differently from the other operators in the area. Boone ran a strictly non-union operation. They paid once a month. New miners had to work two months before receiving any pay. They used the long ton weight, and the ten hour day. They had a company store where the employees were expected to deal. The company had houses for the employees that needed them. Each family had their own garden, and outbuildings so they could keep a cow or chickens. The upkeep was at the company's expense. The company had a generator to furnish power for both the mine and the houses. Mr. Boone's bakery was one of the best, and he shipped bread to all parts of the district. The bakery burned sometime in the 1920's.

Many coal barons made their fortune in West Virginia, and then retired to their home states. Mr. Boone (1867-1956), however, was a native West Virginian, and is buried along with his family in the Jeanette Cemetery at Lookout. The Boone section of the cemetery is completely surrounded by a cut stone wall, that was built by Crockett Creger for the Boone family.

LOOKOUT

Hotel mountain view.

Only the steps remain of the once beautiful hotel.

Thirty-one rooms, electric lights, hot and cold water, a hotel with a view.
COURTESY MRS. PAULINE STONE

LOOKOUT

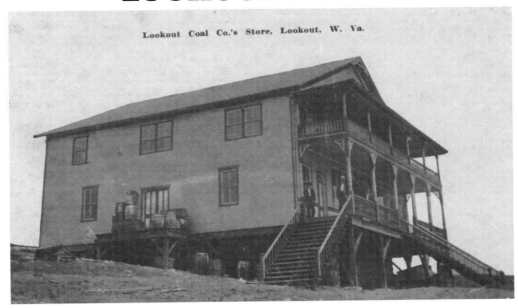

Lookout Coal Co.'s Store, Lookout, W. Va.

Lookout Coal Company store.

Baptist Church, Lookout, W. Va.

Baptist Church. COURTESY MRS. PAULINE STONE

LOOKOUT

Lookout and Divide's grade school building.
COURTESY MRS. PAULINE STONE

D. W. Boone was qualified as a teacher on August 11, 1890. However, his life's work was coal mining. COURTESY MRS. PAULINE STONE

MABEN - Wyoming County:

Mr. H. H. Rogers named this community for John C. Maben, who owned the property. Mr. Rogers had not liked the original name, "Estel." Maben was best know as the W. M. Ritter Lumber Company town.

Mr. Jeff Goode had a small mining operation as well as a lumberyard near Maben. Mr. Goode delivered coal from his mines to local trade and tenants using a team of horses.

The 1933 Department of Mines reported Jeff Goode worked the Fire Creek and Poca No. 6 bed of coal with natural ventilation, produced 2,214 tons, and employed ten men.

Jeff Goode's mine and lumber operations near Maben.

McALPIN - Raleigh County:

Organized and incorporated on July 28, 1908 by James Martin, James Laing, W. T. Green, W. V. Dunlap, and W. H. Warren. John Laing named the community MacAlpin, after his mother's maiden name. Through an error of the U. S. Postal Service, the spelling for the town became McAlpin, but the mine name was spelled MacAlpin.

The town of McAlpin at one time had a YMCA that contained a bowling alley, reading rooms, and a barber shop. Movies were shown at the McAlpin Auditorium. The company store contained dry goods, meats, clothing, cows, pigs, and chickens. The top story contained coffins, furniture and appliances. A church was built for the community in 1923.

By 1917 MacAlpin Coal Company employed 111 men at three mines and produced 314,148 tons that year.

At the time the company was organized, John Laing was Chief of the Department of Mines. A few years later he resigned the position to become the president of MacAlpin Coal Company. Mr. Laing served as president from 1909 until his death in 1943.

Mark Twain High School.

McALPIN

A very early picture of the MacAlpin Coal Company store. Later an office was added to the upper side of the store building and a butcher shop on the side near the tracks. Circa 1910.
COURTESY NAN WHITLOCK GWINN

McALPIN

A view of McAlpin showing the office and butcher shop addition on the store building. The large house with triple gables was the home of the general manager and superintendent. The house to the right was the doctor's home and office. The bookkeeper's house was on the left.

MEAD POCA - Wyoming County: Mead Pocahontas Coal Company was chartered in 1912 under the leadership of J. C. Sullivan. In the first year of operation, John C. Sullivan and the Mead Pocahontas Coal Company shipped 18,000 tons of coal.

Mead Poca Coal Company was situated at the mine site. Mr. Sullivan named the town Mead Poca, but he made the post office address be Tralee. Mead Poca is now part of the city of Mullens.

The main office building in the center with columns, and Sullivan's mansion on the hill above the office building, are both still standing. To the left of the main building is the company store and clubhouse, with the Guyandotte River in the foreground. Homes of the miners scale the mountain's side.

MEAD POCA

J. C. Sullivan's main office building. The radio tower was used to receive and send coal orders. This picture was made after fire hydrants were installed in 1922.

Downriver, the tipple and Virginian railway coal cars at Elmore coal storage yard.

MEAD POCA

Another view of the tipple near Elmore.

Looking toward Elmore yard and across the Guyandotte River to the main section of town. Notice the radio antenna in the center of the picture with the Sullivan mansion above.

MEAD POCA

Loaded coal cars in Elmore yard.

A miner posed for a picture with a mine motor at the mine entrance.

MEAD POCA

Small houses, uniform in size and style, were built in rows and layered up the mountainside. The tipple is in the background. Miners walked to work, women walked to shop, and children walked to school, as roads and cars were uncommon.

Mead Poca dwellings.

MEAD POCA

The repair shop and a small brick building used for dynamite storage.

Bridge No. 68, Virginian Railway Company - Micajah.

MONTECARLO - Wyoming County: Monticello Smokeless Coal Company and Pinnacle Poca Development Company operated a mine called "Monticello" with a drift entrance and mined the Beckley coal seam. The company used the post office address of Montecarlo. Known records show Montecarlo listed only from 1923 until 1927, at which time it could have been worked out, sold, or had its name changed. The primitive looking tipple gives the appearance of being dated much earlier than 1923.

Upper section of the tipple.

Car repair shop.

MONTECARLO

Showing the aerial rock dump from the upper tipple. The dump bucket is the dark spot between the tall trees.

Upper tipple with part of the company name visible on the side. The track in the foreground is for the man hoist.

MONTECARLO

Lower tipple.

View taken from the upper tipple
showing incline and lower tipple.

MORDUE

MORDUE - Boone County: The post office was opened December 21, 1918 with Albert R. Biddy as Postmaster. Mordue Collieries Company operated here from about that date until 1928. Mordue operated Splint No. 1 & No. 2 with C. C. Lewis as superintendent and E. J. Miller as foreman. They mined the Dorothy bed of coal.

Mordue post office was changed to Kam in 1923, and to Red Dragon in 1929.

The tipple.

Mr. Mordue.

MORDUE

Mordue Collieries tipple.

Typical small house for miners.

MORDUE

NALLEN - Fayette County: The original lumber company here was owned by Peter Carroll of Charleston and managed by his son-in-law, J. I. Nallen. In 1916 a double band M-11 mill was erected, and Nallen became the site of the largest hardwood mill in the world. The Wilderness Lumber Company occupied the only level land in town for the sawmill, planing mill, lumber yard, and the railroad.

The History of Fayette County (1926) reported that houses for the employees and their families were built in rows up the steep hillsides. The mill furnished electric power to the town. Water was piped to the houses, and some had steam heat. The large company building housed the U. S. Post Office and the company store. Nearby were the horse stables, locomotive barn, truck garages, and machine shops. The town had a barber shop, company doctor, veterinarian, boarding house, church, bowling alley, and a four-room elementary school. Meadow River, flowing through the town, provided swimming and fishing in the summer, and ice skating in the winter. On the other side of the river, in Nicholas County, were apartment buildings, clothing and grocery stores, theater, lodge hall, service station, soda fountain, and the Methodist church.

The mill closed in 1967 and today little remains of the old lumber town.

Pete and Bud Sovine, miners of a small local mine which furnished coal for the Wilderness Lumber Company and the town of Nallen. The home of Harmon G. Young is behind the picket fence. In the distance is the small building where movies were shown. ALL PHOTOGRAPHS OF NALLEN ARE COURTESY OF JANET CHILDERS

NALLEN

View of Nallen.

Nallen company store.

Wilderness Lumber Company log loader.

NALLEN

Free to roam, the pig and the car.

Mill pond and machine shop.

PAGE - Fayette County: Located on Loup Creek and the Virginian Railroad, in the Kanawha district. Earliest settlement was built here by Andrew Lykens in 1798. Also known as Kincaid, the town site was bought from Lykens by James Kincaid around 1830. The name was changed to Page in 1902 for W. N. Page, head of the Loup Creek Colliery Company that was located here.

The 1904 Annual Department of Mines reported several openings had been made and coke ovens built, but there was no record of coal being shipped by that date. F. P. Mills was superintendent of the new operations.

Loup Creek Colliery Company became one of the biggest operations in Fayette County.

Company store at Page, later destroyed by fire on March 2, 1947. COURTESY FLORENCE PAINTER

PEMBERTON

Ragland Coal Company tipple.

PEMBERTON - Raleigh County: Ragland Coal Company was organized by C. H. Mead around 1923. The 1924 Department of Mines reported a slope mine at Pemberton with William Yates, superintendent and Richard Martin, mine foreman. 99,966 tons of coal were produced that year.

Miners' homes at Pemberton.

PHILLIPS - Raleigh County: Pemberton Coal & Coke Company operated a mine here, as well as in Big Stick and Affinity, as early as 1918. Pemberton reported that in 1924 all of their mines produced 370,877 tons of coal.

Store and office at Pemberton Coal & Coke Company.

Miners' homes at Phillips.

PHILLIPS

Residence of mine foreman - Pemberton Coal & Coke Company.

John Laing, Chief of the Department of Mines, reported in the 1910 issue the following comments regarding wages and strikes.

"The average price received by pick miners throughout the state per gross tons to run-of-mine coal was 44 cents as against 43 cents for the year 1909. Each pick miner produced on an average 1,304.4 tons per year, being an increase of 193.2 tons more per man employed than the previous year. The average yearly wages per pick miner employed was $573.94, an increase over the preceding year of $92.77.

There were strikes at twenty mines in the state during the year, involving 2,225 employees, causing a loss of 315 days work to the miners at which the strikes occurred and a financial loss to the employees of $100,367.25 in wages, and a loss of $15,374.93 to the operators of the mines, making an aggregate loss, caused by the strikes, of $115,742.18.

The operators won seven of the strikes, and the employees won eleven, the other two being compromised."

PICKSHIN - Raleigh County:

The Pickshin Coal Company began operations in 1917 and used the post office at Besoco. Frank McHugh was superintendent and James Hastie was mine foreman. The Beckley coal seam was mined with thirty-nine workers; the mines operated 62 days that year. Their production was 9,942 tons, which were shipped on the Virginian Railway. Pickshin Coal Company operated for approximately 10 years.

Pickshin Coal Company store, unfinished and unpainted. Later the store was painted white.

Clubhouse.

PICKSHIN

Part of the tipple and incline from mine above the railroad tracks. Men are working on the man hoist that climbs the hill on the tracks visible parallel to the incline from the mine. The man hoist carried the miners to the mouth of the mine above.

Repair shop for mine cars and motors.

PICKSHIN

Cut stone building for dynamite storage.

Drift mouth mine entrance.

PICKSHIN

Horse and wagon pass by Pickshin homes on a rough road.

Pickshin houses.

PICKSHIN

Dynamite stone building, repair shop, and maintenance building with mine cars.

A section of the tipple.

PICKSHIN

Row houses on a very rocky road.

Pickshin houses.

PICKSHIN

PICKSHIN

Monitors carried the coal from the mine to the tipple. They operated with a drum holding the cable, so that as one came down, the other monitor was pulled up.

Mine entrance.

QUINNIMONT

QUINNIMONT - Fayette County: The town of Quinnimont was established in 1873 by Joseph L. Beury. He shipped the first coal out on the C & O Railway in September 1873.

After the building of Stretcher's Neck Tunnel by the railroad, coal mines could be opened. In 1870, the Quinnimont Charter Oak & Iron Company was organized for the purpose of building and operating an iron furnace. The furnace manufactured pig iron and operated for three years. A boarding house was established for the iron furnace employees.

Numerous mines were operated in the area by several companies. Quinnimont, being located near the junction of the Piney River Railroad and the Laurel Creek Branch Road, soon became a railroad center. It was a prosperous little community with a store, post office, church and two schools.

The home of one of Joseph L. Beury's daughters, Mrs. Emma Galladett. Joe Lawton later lived in the house. It was razed about 1960. The three story mansion had a ballroom on the second floor. COURTESY KATHERINE WATKINS

QUINNIMONT

Old store and post office.

All that remains of the old schoolhouse, that was later used as a residential dwelling for several families.

RALCO - Raleigh County: Another of the Sullivan Interests, Raleigh Fire Creek Coal Company was operating the slope mine "Battleship" in 1921. They named their community Ralco, but used the post office at Jonben.

Raleigh Fire Creek Coal Company tipple.

Homes near the tipple.

RALCO

A very primitive loading tipple with incline ramp from the mine at a lower elevation.

Miners' homes in Ralco.

RALCO

Ralco homes with company store at right foreground.

Homes and coal houses.

RALCO

This building probably housed the mules used in the mine, with the upper section used for hay storage.

This building had sliding doors and no windows; it was probably used for dynamite storage.

RALCO

Power plant for Ralco.

A very roughly constructed house used by loggers prior to miners. Housing for loggers was usually for short term work and quality housing was not built.

RALCO

Raleigh Fire Creek Coal Company clubhouse.

Ralco residence with a cow grazing in the yard, and a wash tub hanging on a small building.

RALCO

The tipple and incline ramp. The mine cars were pulled up and dumped (tipped) into coal cars below. This was necessary because the coal seam was lower than the tipple. The electric plant is on the left and a mine repair shop on the right.

Drift mouth of the mine.

RALEIGH - Raleigh County:

Raleigh Coal & Coke Company was situated on Piney Creek, a tributary of the New River, and on the Piney Creek branch of the C & O Railroad. Raleigh Coal & Coke was the first major mining operation in the county. The company was founded in 1898 under the leadership of Logan M. Bullitt, of Philadelphia. He was succeeded by Funstum Lacado, of Lynchburg, Virginia, and next in line was T. J. Morgan from Ohio. Mr. Morgan brought many of his workers from Ohio, and by 1901 they had established a settlement on one of the hills overlooking the valley and mines. This area of Raleigh is still known as Ohio Hill.

The symbol of the "Black Knight in Armor," the first trademark ever attached by a coal company to its product, was chosen by the vice president of Raleigh Coal & Coke, A. A. Liggett. The "Black Knight" was intended to dramatize the selling of coal by drawing on the tradition of the Middle Ages.

The first buildings erected in Raleigh were a store and a large boarding house. Slowly, the community grew up around them on the swampy bottom that had been cleared by a lumber company. The first houses constructed by the company were built there by "Captain" Wells.

It was said that the greatest growth of the company and community was during the era of Colonel Ernest Chilson, vice president from 1906 to his death in 1931. When Chilson came to Raleigh, the coal firm employed some 150 men and produced about 15,000 tons a year. Shortly before his death, the employee figure had grown to 900 and annual production was over the 1,000,000 ton mark, making Raleigh Coal one of the biggest firms in the field. Colonel Chilson was a leader in all Raleigh County civic projects. He was responsible for starting the Black Knight Country Club and Golf Course on land the company owned.

The first doctor at Raleigh was Dr. James Gooch, who came to the community when the first mine was opened in 1898. He was succeeded by Dr. W. A. Campbell, who was followed in 1903 by Dr. W. W. Hume. Both Dr. Campbell and Dr. Hume moved to Beckley. Considered to be the dean of "company doctors", Dr. M. C. Banks came to Raleigh in 1904 and served this community for several generations. The sanitation phase of the job at Raleigh was never overlooked by Dr. Banks. For years he campaigned each spring against typhoid and dysentery, and residents of the community were vaccinated twice a year.

RALEIGH

Electric power plant and the manpower to operate 66,000 volts of electricity for Raleigh. COURTESY JACK MAYS

All that remains today of the power plant that once supplied the company, all the mines, the residents of Raleigh, and part of Beckley with power.

RALEIGH

The Black Knight Country Club was the large building in the center; the home of J. P. White, company president, is to the left; and P. M. Anderson's home is on the right. In May 1928, 125 men met and formed the Black Knight Country Club. The first officers were Ernest Chilson, president; J. L. Bumgardner, chairman of the board; and Clifford Mutter, secretary-treasurer. COURTESY JACK MAYS

RALEIGH

The home of Raleigh's Boy Scouts of America No. 2, located behind the old company store. In 1914 or 1915, a group of boys met in the home of Robert Thomson, and began operating according to the program of the "Boy Brigade", brought over from England. The Raleigh Boy Scouts were chartered as Troop No. 2 in May 1916, with R. B. Holmes as scoutmaster. COURTESY JACK MAYS

RALEIGH

The tipple ramp, the black school just in front of the ramp, and to the right, the Dixie Hotel. The Dixie Hotel housed the black ball players brought in for the company's team. The ballpark was located on Route 3 where the old Raleigh Motor Sales building now sits. COURTESY JACK MAYS

Raleigh Coke & Coal Company store as it looks today, with boarded windows and up for sale. This store replaced a three story frame building that was destroyed by fire.

RHODELL

RHODELL - Raleigh County: Rhodell Coal Company was founded in 1907, incorporated in 1939, and named for one of its founders, I. J. Rhodes. Prior to this time, the community around the coal mines had been called Rhodesdale. The E. C. Minter Coal Company opened the Frances mine in 1921 and the Minter mine, in 1923. In 1922 the mine "Frances" produced 30,150 tons and mined from the Stonecoal seam. In 1933 the superintendent was A. K. Minter, and the mine foreman was W. M. Stewart.

Both the E. C. Minter Coal Company and Rhodell Coal Company were under the umbrella of Western Pocahontas Corporation.

Rhodell Coal Company store and office.

Store and Office, RHODELL COAL CO., Rhodell, W. Va.

RHODELL

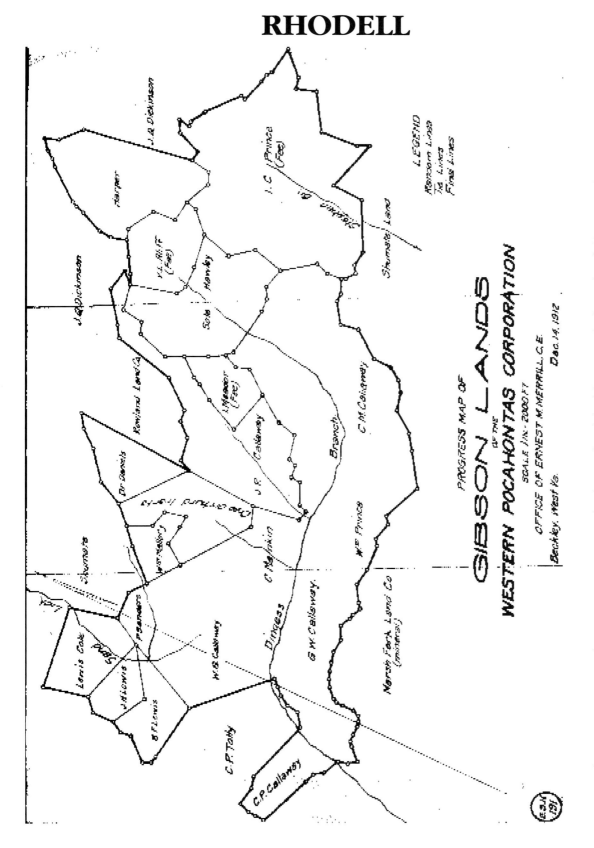

The Western Pocahontas Corporation had vast land holdings including the following that are featured in this book: C. H. Mead Coal Company, Rhodell Coal Company, East Gulf Coal Company, E. C. Minter Coal Company, and the Jeff Goode Mine.

RHODELL

Tipple loading fifty-five ton Virginian Railway cars.

A view of the tipple.

RHODELL

A three room miners' house which was used for the clubhouse for the Rhodell Coal Company.

A view of Rhodell.

RHODELL

A section of Rhodell.

Rhodell housing.

RHODELL

Tipple. The sixteen ton mine cars were pulled here and dumped into coal cars.

Air shaft and fan.

RHODELL

Mine entrance for Rhodell Coal Company.

Homes along the track.

RHODELL

A view of Rhodell.

E. C. Minter Coal Company tipple at Rhodell.

RHODELL

Small houses near tipple.

E. C. Minter Coal Company's generating plant, repair shop, and emergency siren.

RHODELL

Homes in
Rhodell.

RHODELL

Tipple of the E. C. Minter Coal Company.

SLAB FORK

SLAB FORK - Raleigh County: Slab Fork Coal Company was formed in April 1907, by G. H. Caperton, W. Gaston Caperton, J. F. Brown, Malcolm Jackson, E. D. Knight, and Gory Hogg. Slab Fork leased 4,585 acres from the Beaver Land Company and W. Gaston Caperton moved into the wilderness as general manager of the new company. He remained in that position until 1928, when he became president, succeeding his older brother, George Henry Caperton. The brothers worked closely together from the early 1890's. The Capertons opened the first mine in what was later to become the Winding Gulf District. At that time the only means of transportation in and out of Slab Fork was either by foot or horseback over bridle paths.

The Capertons had the distinction of loading the first railway car of coal in Raleigh County from their Winding Gulf coal fields. In 1907, the Virginian Railway made its first connection from Deepwater in Fayette County to Sewell's Point, Virginia. With the completion of this line, Slab Fork Coal Company had completed its construction and shipped the first train load of coal over the line. The first tipple of wooden construction was replaced in 1926 by a modern preparation plant.

The annual output from this property grew from 250,000 tons in 1910 to approximately 650,000 tons in 1956.

Today several homes remain in Slab Fork, but the coal industry is gone.

General view of Slab Fork Coal Company.

SLAB FORK

Slab Fork Coal Company No. 10 opened on Winding Gulf Creek near Tams. The mine, No. 10, was commonly referred to as located on the "Tams side of the mountain" from the town of Slab Fork. The Austin Black plant is on the left of the preparation plant, with storage tanks on the right.

The church for the black community.

SLAB FORK

The parking lot, office, and bath house for the operations of No. 10.

Only the concrete foundations of No. 10 remain in this 1991 photo.

SLAB FORK

Slab Fork Coal Company No. 10. Cars broken loose and derailed at tipple area. Circa 1975.

STOTESBURY

STOTESBURY - Raleigh County: E. E. White, coal company president, opened the mine, naming the community Stotesbury in honor of Edward T. Stotesbury, president of Beaver Coal Company. Mr. White opened this mine in 1910, one year after he opened the Glen White mine. The community of Stotesbury was built with the high quality of employee housing seen in his town of Glen White.

In 1925, Mr. White sold his mines and returned to his home state of Pennsylvania. Stotesbury had a hospital, doctors, theater, amusement hall and other recreational facilities. In the heart of the southern coal fields, this town that once had more than 2,000 residents, had less than 200 in 1995. The mines shut down in 1958.

Emergency hospital in mine.

STOTESBURY

The Soldiers Monument - 1917 World War I Memorial was erected by the E. E. White Coal Company and features the names of coal miners who served in the war.

Fan house - No. 5 mine.

SYLVESTER - Boone County:

The Webb Coal Company located near here, used Ferndale for the train freight address, and Garrison as their post office address. Production started around 1910 for this company, with John Holmes as superintendent. In 1920 they mined the Coalburg seam and produced 92,298 tons. A lengthy strike in 1921-23 dropped their production to 52,967 tons. By 1926, they were producing 228,892 tons, employed 170 men and averaged 265 work days.

The following picture was made during a union strike when the Company evicted all the striking miners. Men hired by the company (called "thugs" by the miners) came through the camp, picking up furniture and belongings of the families and setting them on the road. Ernie Williams drove about in a horse drawn wagon and hauled their possessions to this property in Sylvester owned by Parley Koon. This was home for over a year and a half to the miners and their families.

Serving as their homes for this year and a half in Sylvester were regulation army squad tents, loaned by the U. S. Army. Tents were issued depending on the size of the family. My source for this picture and story, Robert (Buster) Burnside, of Dry Creek, said his family had two tents. When questioned how the family managed to survive financially, he said that they had gardens and received some assistance from the UMWA.

The 1933 Department of Mines reported that the West Virginia Penitentiary operated a shaft mine at Moundsville. The superintendent was Rex Radar, and mine foreman was Loe Pack. They operated the Pittsburgh No. 8 seam of coal. 11,918 tons was mined for their own use and none was shipped on railroads.

SYLVESTER

Mr. Burnside is the little boy near the center, in the front row, with his sister directly behind him. To the best of his knowledge, of the people in the photograph, only he, his sister, and two others are still living. COURTESY BUSTER BURNSIDE

TOMMY CREEK

- Raleigh County: Around 1920 a drift mine was opened by the Tommy Creek Coal Company, located near Rhodell; it used the post office at Amigo. Phillip Konrad served as superintendent and K. S. McClanahan as mine foreman. Tommy Creek employed sixty men and mined 38,261 tons from the Beckley seam. The coal was mined by mining machines, runners, helpers, and inside and outside laborers. No pick miners were used.

The steel construction remains of the new tipple of Tommy Creek Coal Company that burned down. The tipple for the lower seam is in the foreground.

TOMMY CREEK

Miners' homes.

Clubhouse.

TRALEE

TRALEE - Wyoming County: Located in the Barkers Ridge district. The Harty Coal Company and Barkers Creek Coal Company operated on Barkers Creek under the leadership of the Sullivan interests. Mr. Sullivan named the post office Tralee after his homeland, Tralee, England.

Harty Coal Company store and office, located on Barkers Creek.

Harty Coal Company tipple.

TRALEE - HARTY COAL COMPANY

Overlooking Tralee. Tipple can be seen in background with houses clustered around it. The amusement hall, the large building, is in the center beside Barkers Creek.

Break time for the miners. Water tank and work area for the mines.

TRALEE - BARKERS CREEK COAL COMPANY

Tralee houses.

Power house.

TRALEE - BARKERS CREEK COAL COMPANY

Tipple and incline leading to top of the mountain to mouth of mine.

Some of the miners' homes with tipple in the background.

TRALEE - BARKERS CREEK COAL COMPANY

Tipple and incline.

A section of the tipple.

TRALEE - BARKERS CREEK COAL COMPANY

Houses along the railroad tracks and Barkers Creek.

Clubhouse.

TRALEE - BARKERS CREEK COAL COMPANY

Part of the tipple operations and a view of Tralee.

Four room hip roof houses along the railroad tracks. The horse drawn wagon was the transportation of the day.

VANWOOD - Raleigh County:

Another part of the Sullivan interests, the Wood Sullivan Coal Company started production around 1916 or 1917. The mine, community, and post office were named Vanwood. In 1917 the Fire Creek seam of coal was mined and produced 47,487 long tons of coal.

One miner, John Koss, was killed in a slate fall in 1917. He was Hungarian, married with one child, and had five years of mining experience.

Wood Sullivan Coal Company.

Vanwood miners' homes.

148

VANWOOD

Wood Sullivan Coal Company tipple.

Loaded C & O cars - notice the two sizes of cars.

VANWOOD

Repair shop.

Mine cars entering tipple to be dumped.

VANWOOD

Another view of tipple and incline.

Mine motor and miner at entrance to the mine.

VANWOOD

Vanwood houses.

VANWOOD

The track for the monitor. The monitor carried coal from the mines. A monitor is entering the covered incline in this photograph.

The monitor.

WHIPPLE

WHIPPLE - Fayette County: Whipple, situated on a branch of Loup Creek near the corporate limits of Oak Hill, was named in honor of William Whipple of Portsmouth, N. H.

Justus Collins acquired the property, located the shaft, and developed the Whipple mine. The Whipple company store was built by Mr. Collins for the Whipple Colliery Company. In 1906 Collins sold the Whipple mines to the New River Company. Whipple was one of a group of six similar producers of the famous White Oak Smokeless coal, the product of the New River Company of MacDonald, West Virginia. MacDonald is now part of Mount Hope. The store was occupied by White Oak Fuel Company, and later by the New River Coal Company.

Justus Collins' Whipple Company Store as it looks today.

WINDING GULF

- Raleigh County: In 1910 Justus Collins opened the Winding Gulf mine on the Virginian Railroad. In 1929 Mr. Collins consolidated his holdings under the name of Winding Gulf Collieries. The principal companies involved were the Louisville Coal and Coke Company at Goodwill, the Winding Gulf Colliery Company, and the Superior Pocahontas Coal Company. The Smokeless Fuel Company was established as the sales agency.

A view of Winding Gulf.

Baseball field.

WINDING GULF

Tipple and power house.

Our English Heritage

In Great Britain, a *collier* is a coal miner or a ship for carrying coal, or any of its crew. A *colliery* is a coal mine and its building and equipment.

WINONA - Fayette County:
In 1893 William Masters and Son opened the Masters mine on Keeneys Creek, mining the Sewell seam with 40 inches of coal. Masters soon sold to John C. Campbell and others of the Beechwood Company on the New River, and the name was changed to Smokeless Coal Company. The superintendent was John C. Campbell; William Hall was mine boss. The mine employed 63 people.

On Keeneys Creek, W. F. Boone opened the Boone mine. The Dubree mine was opened in 1893. The Rosedale mine was opened in 1907 by the Rothwell Coal Company. Rothwell opened the Quarrier mine in 1897, but only operated it until 1902.

By 1910 Smokeless was owned by Keeney's Creek Colliery Company, employed 102 people, and produced 80,559 tons of coal for the year. This was a drift mine located on the Keeneys Creek branch of the C & O Railroad. Lee Long was manager, and Thomas H. Seacrist was mine foreman. By 1914, J. Wade Bell was superintendent. In 1918 the Smokeless mine was owned by Maryland New River Company, who operated it for several years. Maryland New River also purchased the Boone, Dubree, and Rosedale mines on Keeneys Creek.

Winona developed as a mining town on the branch of the C & O Railroad. The small town is located on the headwaters of Keeneys Creek in the mountainous Nuttall District. The entire site on which Winona was built was formerly owned by Robert M. Holliday, Sr., a farmer and pioneer settler. The Winona post office was named for Winona Gwinn, oldest daughter of William Gwinn. R. E. Deitz was the postmaster in 1892; the first post office was located in the old store building of Gwinn & Deitz.

As the mines around Winona grew, so did the community life. Churches, a school, and civic clubs were organized. The First Baptist Church was organized in 1895. The land to erect the church building was purchased for $10.00 from the Smokeless Coal Company about 1910. This church closed its doors in April 1990 with only three members remaining in the congregation. A Methodist Episcopal church was started in 1894; the church was erected in 1906. Mrs. William Nuttall furnished the funds for building the Presbyterian church at Dubree during the early 1890's. A Catholic church was built in Winona in 1906.

The first school was a one-room building located behind the Hall & Stemple store. When the school opened in this building in 1895, the teacher was a Mr. Clay. There was an enrollment of 75 pupils during the first term. Three rooms were added in 1897.

The Masonic lodge was chartered in 1888 with a membership of 160. Other local organizations included the Knights of Pythias, Order of United American Men, Improved Order of Red Men, Independent Order of Odd Fellows, Loyal Order of Moose, and Eastern Star.

WINONA

The coal companies -- Ballenger, Smokeless and Rothwell Coal Company -- all built company stores. A drug store, Walker, Quesenbury & Company opened in 1895, but ceased business in 1900. Shops originally included a dry goods store, meat market, pool room, blacksmith shop, barber shop, millinery, and grocery store. The shops changed hands many times, and have all since closed. The first moving picture theater was opened by George Ash and was later destroyed by fire. The lower part of the Masonic Hall was next used as a movie theater.

The Winona National Bank, with capital of $25,000, was organized on September 17, 1905. The first president was Lee Long, and the first cashier was W. W. Michael. The building was a one-story brick building, trimmed with cut stone and having a solid rock foundation. The vault was built of solid concrete, was twenty-two inches thick, and weighed over 2,000 pounds. It was also equipped with the latest improved lock, a Mosler thribble time lock, and a Mosler door. The Winona National Bank was later moved to Gauley Bridge.

A hotel was in operation in Winona for several years, as well as numerous boarding houses.

Smokeless Coal Company.

PAWAMA

PARTIAL VIEW OF POWAMA COAL & COKE CO. CAMP SHOWING NORFOLK & WESTERN AND VIRGINIAN RAILROADS AND MACADAM HIGHWAY

Notice the variant spelling of Pawama. COURTESY ERNEST F. REYNOLDS

163

Today in the Coal Fields

Today, not many buildings, none of the tipples, and few communities remain of the towns included in this book. These last photographs are reminders of a bygone era.

Semet Solvay Company, Harewood - 1997.

Princess Dorothy Coal Company Store, Eunice - razed in 1991.

164

Coke Ovens at Powellton - 1997.

Westmoreland Coal Company, MacAlpin - 1991

AFFINITY

Affinity - 1991. Once a thriving coal community.

BIBLIOGRAPHY

Conley, Phil, *History of West Virginia Coal Industry,* Charleston, WV., 1960.

Feller, John W. "Jack", *Mullens, West Virginia,* St. Albans, WV., 1993.

History of Fayette County, by Fayette County Chamber of Commerce, 1993.

Holliday, Robert Kelvin, *A Portrait of Fayette County West Virginia,* Fayette Tribune, Inc., Oak Hill, WV., 1960.

Peters, J. T., & Carden, H. B., *History of Fayette County West Virginia,* Charleston, WV., 1926.

Tams, W. P., Jr., *The Smokeless Coal Fields of West Virginia: A Brief History,* West Virginia University Press, Morgantown, WV., 1963.

Wood, Jim, *Raleigh County West Virginia,* Beckley, WV., 1994.

Various articles from the *Beckley Post Herald* and *Raleigh Register.*

West Virginia, Annual Report of the Department of Mines, 1895-1933.

ABOUT THE AUTHOR

Mary Legg Stevenson was born on Muddy Creek Mountain in Greenbrier County, but has lived in Beckley since early childhood. She attended Beckley schools, and was employed by the City of Beckley, Gates Engineering Company and the Magistrate Clerk's office.

Mary served as president of the Raleigh County Historical Society for five years, and is an active member of the Beckley Presbyterian Church, the Order of Eastern Star, and the Beckley Area Concert Association.

She has previously written two pictorial history books, *From Affinity to Winding Gulf,* and *From Ameagle to Wingrove.*

Mary and her husband Daniel reside in Bradley. They enjoy traveling, walking, cooking, and reading. They share five children and four grandchildren.

Dan and Mary Stevenson
COURTESY DR. WILLIAM McLEAN

Index

Affinity, 166
Adams, Bud, 12
Amherst Coal Company, 11
Amick, Stark, 5
Amigo Smokeless Coal Company, 2
Anderson, P. M., 113
Ashley, Elmer, 159
Backman, Val, 29
Bailey Wood Coal Company, 21, 70
Ballenger Coal Company, 158
Banks, Dr. M. C., 111
Barkers Creek Coal Company, 14, 137
Beaver Land Company, 127, 131
Beckley Smokeless Coal Company, 7
Beechwood Company, 157
Bell, J. Wade, 157
Beury, Joseph L., 8, 10, 19, 102
Biddy, Albert, 80
Blake, Henry, 44
Blake, J. C., 70
Boone, Andrew, 59
Boone, D. W., 19, 59, 62
Boone, James, 29
Boone, W. F., 157
Booth, William, 86
Bragg, Leota, 159
Brown, J. F., 127
Bryant, C. B., 70
Bullitt, Logan M., 111
Bumgardner, J. L., 113
Burnside, Robert (Buster), 134
C. H. Mead Coal Company, *see* Mead Coal
    Company, C.H.
Campbell, Dr. W. A., 111
Campbell, John C., 157
Caperton, G. H., 10, 127
Caperton, W. Gaston, 127
Carroll, Pete, 87
Cavendish, J. F., 59
Chilson, Col. Ernest, 111, 113
Collins, Justus, 154, 155
Cooper, John, 19
Crickmer, Walter B., 68
DeHart, Herman, 159
DeHart, Ida Kessler, 159
Deitz, R. E., 157
Dice, Bob, 159
Douglas Coal Company, 32
Dunlap, W. V., 64
E. C. Minter Coal Company *see* Minter Coal
    Company, E. C.
E. E. White Coal Company, *see* White Coal
    Company, E. E.

East Gulf Coal Company, 44, 117
Eastern Gas & Fuel, 3
Electro Metallurgical Company, 1, 33
Elkhorn Piney Coal Company, 3
Evans, Mr., 159
Faith Smokeless Coal Company, 21, 27, 28, 86
Flaherty, Mrs. Eugenia Woodville, 159
Forbes, Julia A., 8
Galladett, Emma, 102
Garvey, Bill, 159
Gooch, Dr. James, 111
Goode, Jeff, 63, 117
Guthrie, Augustis S., 10
Green, W. T., 64
Gunnoe, Cosby, 19
Gwinn, William, 157
Gwinn, Winona, 157
Hall, William, 157
Harty Coal Company, 14, 137
Hastie, James, 94
Henry, P. H., 29
Hill, Meredith, 159
Hogg, Gory, 127
Holliday, Robert M., Sr., 157
Holmes, John, 133
Holmes, R. B., 114
Hopkins, A. S. J., 11
Hornbrook, John B., 57
Hume, Dr. W. W., 111
Hyman, G. W., 34
Itmann Coal Company, 54
Jackson, Malcolm, 127
Johnson, Dr. George, 68
Johnson, George, 159
Keeneys Creek Colliery Co., 157
Kincaid, James, 90
Knight, E. D., 127
Konrad, Phillip, 135
Koppers Coal Company, 3
Koss, John, 148
Lacado, Funstum, 111
Laing, James, 64
Laing, John, 10, 64, 93
Leckie Fire Creek Coal Company, 32
Lewis, C. C., 80
Liggett, A. A., 111
Lilly, Prince E., 57
Lillybrook Coal Company, 2, 32, 57
Long, Lee, 157, 158
Lookout Coal & Coke Company, 59, 61
Louisville Coal & Coke Company, 155
Loup Creek Colliery Company, 3, 90
Lykens, Andrew, 90

Index

Maben, John C., 63
MacAlpin Coal Company, 64, 65
Mann, Isaac, T. 54
Manufacturers & Consumers Coal, 29, 30
Martin, James, 64
Martin, Richard, 91
Maryland New River Co., 157, 159
Masters, William, 157
Matewan Affair, 162
McClanahan, K. S., 135
McHugh, Frank, 94
McKendree Hospital, 19
Mead, C. H., 21, 27, 28, 70, 86, 91
Mead Coal Company, C. H., 21, 117
Mead Poca Coal Company, 71
Mead Pocahontas Coal Company, 14, 71
Michael, W. M., 158
Michigan Coal Company, 29, 31
Mill Creek Coal & Coke Company, 8
Miller, D. W., 7
Miller, E. J., 80
Mills, F. P., 90
Minter, A. K., 14, 116
Minter Coal Company, E. C., 2, 116, 117
Minter, E. C., IX, 7
Monticello Smokeless Coal Co., 77
Mordue Collieries Company, 80, 81
Mordue, Mr., 80
Morgan, T. J., 111
Mutter, Clifford, 113
Nallen, J. I., 87
New River Coal Company, 8, 154
New River Export Smokeless Coal Company, 29
Nuttall, Mrs. William, 157
Pack, Loe, 133
Page, W. N., 90
Pawama, 162, 163
Pemberton Coal & Coke Co., 92
Pickshin Coal Company, 14, 94
Pinnacle Poca Development Company, 77
Pocahontas Fuel Company, 54
Powellton, 165
Princess Dorothy Coal Co., 164
Pugh, Roy, 159
Quinn, Thomas, 11
Quinnimont Charter Oak & Iron Company, 102
Radar, Rex, 133
Ragland Coal Company, 21, 91
Raleigh Coal & Coke Company, 111
Raleigh Fire Creek Coal Co., 14, 104
Raleigh Wyoming Coal Company, 14, 34, 35
Repass, I. R., 86

Rhodell Coal Company, 116, 117
Rhodes, I. J., 116
Ritter Lumber Company, 34, 54, 63
Rogers, H. H., VIII, 34, 35, 36, 63
Rogers, Worthington, 159
Rothwell Coal Company, 157, 158
Seacrist, Thomas H., 157
Semet Solvay Company, 164
Sims, James W., 29
Slab Fork Coal Company, 127
Smith Pocahontas Coal Company, 14
Smith, John W., 86
Smokeless Coal Company, 157, 158
Smokeless Fuel Company, 155
Sovine, Bud, 87
Sovine, Pete, 87
Stevens, G. W., 44
Stewart, W. M., 116
Stotesbury, Edward T., 131
Sullivan, J. C., 14, 71, 72, 137, 148
Superior Pocahontas Coal Company, 155
Tabor, Charlie, 20
Tams, Major W. P., IX
Tams, W. P., Jr., 85
Thermo Pocahontas Coal Company, 12, 13
Thomas, P. C., 44
Thompson, Bob, 5
Tommy Creek Coal Company, 135
Union Carbide Metals Company, 1
Warren, W. H., 10, 64
Webb Coal Company, 133
West Virginia Eagle Coal Company, 1
Western Pocahontas Coal Company, 21, 44, 116, 117
Westmoreland Coal Co., 165
Whipple Colliery Company, 154
Whipple, William, 154
White Coal Company, E. E., 42
White, E. E., 42, 131
White, J. P., 113
White Oak Fuel Company, 154
Wilderness Lumber Company, 87
Williams, Ernie, 133
Willson Aluminum Company, 1
Wilton Smokeless Coal Company, 55, 56
Winding Gulf Colliery Company, 155
Winona National Bank, 158, 159, 161
Wirt, John, 20
Wood Sullivan Coal Company, 14, 148
Wood, Dr. Joseph A., 2
Yates, William, 91
Young, Harmon G., 87